DREAM THE BOLDEST DREAMS

And Other Lessons of Life

JOHNNETTA B. COLE

LONGSTREET PRESS
Atlanta, Georgia

Published by LONGSTREET PRESS, INC.
A subsidiary of Cox Newspapers,
A subsidiary of Cox Enterprises, Inc.
2140 Newmarket Parkway
Suite 122
Marietta, Georgia 30067

Printed in the United States of America

1st printing 1997

Library of Congress Card Catalog Number: 97-71932

ISBN: 1-56352-424-4

Film supplied by OGI, Forest Park, GA
Book and jacket design by Burtch Bennett Hunter

Jacket photograph by Peggy Madkins
Book photographs courtesy of Spelman College.

*This one is for my husband, Art Robinson,
who always understands and supports my boldest dreams.*

CONTENTS

COUNSEL

Never acquire a lifestyle you're willing to sell your soul to keep.

❖

The Good Lord will help those who help themselves. So get on with your self-help program.

It is far better to learn to walk fully in your own footprints than to force a fit into someone else's.

Never underestimate the power of human empathy as a way to understand the plight of one who is different from you.

3

It's best to leave while people still want you to stay.

❖

Never let an injustice become yesterday's news.

❖

We each need to admit when we are wrong and be humble when we're right.

All of us must eat to live; too many of us live to eat — indeed, the latter program can kill you.

Because there is no evidence that there is another earth somewhere, we sure need to take better care of the one we have.

Harold E. Rhynie

GENEROSITY

What you give ought to be in direct relationship to what you've received. If you have been blessed with a great deal, then you have a lot of giving to do.

❖

The greatest reward in doing for others is in having done so.

To the expression "put your money where your mouth is," we would do well to add the request that each of us put some money where our hearts are — give to the causes you care about.

❖

There is an important difference between what we need and what we want. Therein can lie the distinction between necessity and gluttony.

Anyone who ever gets to the top of a field doesn't get there by him or herself. And once there, you should not forget the responsibility to help others join you.

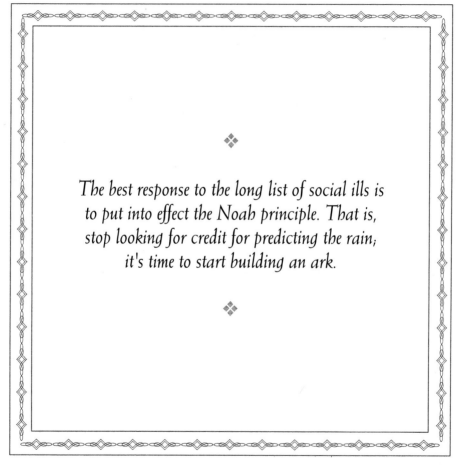

The best response to the long list of social ills is to put into effect the Noah principle. That is, stop looking for credit for predicting the rain; it's time to start building an ark.

There is an exquisite paradox about giving to others. You always end up receiving so much more than you give.

The ultimate expression of generosity is not in giving of what you have, but in giving of who you are.

There are times when the best gift we can give to someone we truly care about is solitude.

The greatest expressions of generosity often come from those who have the fewest things to give.

WOMEN

The problem with a woman standing behind her man is she can't see where she's going.

❖

For us women folks, the distance between where we've been and where we're going is surely determined by the speed at which we insist on moving.

*For every hero in this world,
there's at least one shero.*

❖

*No woman should be against men, but every
woman should be for women.*

*If you've seen one woman,
you haven't seen us all.*

❖

*It has been said: If you educate a man,
you educate a man. If you educate a woman,
you educate a nation.*

The higher the pay, the less likely it's going to be called women's work.

❖

Think what a better world we would have if women folks raised feminist sons.

Men may well be from Mars and we women folks from Venus. But we have got to figure out how to live better with each other right here on earth.

The main reason a woman's work is never done is because a man doesn't pitch in to help finish it.

A truly determined woman will succeed in doing what society has determined she is incapable of doing.

Women who do not love themselves can hardly be expected to feel that way about a man.

We could stop a lot of things from falling if we just let women hold up half the sky.

❖

Not every woman wants to be a mother. And no man can be by giving birth to a child. But every woman and every man, too, is capable of expressing a mothering spirit.

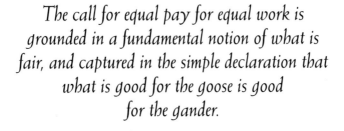

The call for equal pay for equal work is grounded in a fundamental notion of what is fair, and captured in the simple declaration that what is good for the goose is good for the gander.

HARMONY

How much better our world would be if each of us respected difference until difference doesn't make any more difference.

❖

In this complex and highly competitive world of ours, a diverse work force is as much an economic necessity as a moral imperative.

Because freedom is indivisible, pitting one oppression against another harms us all.

❖

One flower never makes a spring. Imagine if we put that Chinese proverb into full force in our American reality.

*If only we could develop an
intolerance for bigotry.*

❖

*Racism, sexism, anti-Semitism, ablism,
and homophobia are learned. So we
can unlearn them. Better yet,
we could just stop teaching them.*

Unfortunately, being a victim of oppression does not immune one from victimizing others.

If what is preached in the world's churches, synagogues, mosques, and temples was practiced by even a quarter of the folks who heard it all said — what a different planet we would have.

We're going to have to learn to live with our differences or share the same fate of destructiveness.

It is far easier to engage in too much or too little of anything than to hit that special place called moderation.

If you are obsessed with trying to keep others in their place, you'll hardly have time to occupy what you think is your own.

It is often said that timing is everything. But could it be that everything is as much about patience as timing?

EDUCATION

If there is anything that we know for sure in the world of education, it's that teachers will get just what they expect from students.

When it comes to education, some good ol' fashion repetition is good for the soul.

Hoarding a good idea is the best way to lose it.

❖

*There is no such thing as an uneducable child,
but there are unteaching teachers.*

A mistake can be a superb teacher of success.

An education that teaches you to understand something about the world has done only half of the assignment. The other half is to teach you to do something about making the world a better place.

*In the words of a Mississippi slave owner:
Knowledge and slavery are incompatible.*

❖

*Education is the single most consistent and
powerful instrument for the advancement of an
individual and a people.*

The first sign of an educated person is that she asks more questions than she delivers answers.

❖

To the African proverb, "She who learns must teach," let us add: She who teaches must continue to learn.

One of the best ways to use one's wisdom is to discover what is in reality common sense.

It is more important to understand what you learned during a given hour than what you did while it passed.

INSPIRATION

Nothing heals as well as hope.

❖

*The beauty of the human mind over the body is
that if you can't run, you may walk; if you
can't walk, you can crawl; if you can't
crawl — stay still and imagine getting there.*

*Some of the very best ideas begin in our hearts.
Then we can send them to our heads for a kind
of intellectual affirmation.*

*Each of us has the power of transforming the
ordinary into the extraordinary — the everyday
into the special. To do so is far more rewarding
than going the other way around.*

GROWTH

Once you have no more questions to ask, the answer to the fundamental one — are you living fully — is a resounding no!

When we go out looking for ourselves, it's amazing how we find others.

Have you noticed that the most fulfilled people you know are the ones who are constantly in search of what they don't know?

❖

When things are done consistently the same old way, the same old results can be expected.

❖

Two questions you had better ask yourself —
and make sure you get them in the right order:
Where am I going? Who am I going with?

❖

The declaration that the sun always rises in the East and sets in the West is of little importance to one who challenges the existence of the sun.

What often stops our aspirations from turning into real possibilities is a lack of belief and a shortage of effort.

❖

Sure there's something far worse than going around in circles: It's going in a straight line that's pointed straight down.

Show me someone content with mediocrity and I'll show you someone destined for failure.

❖

Learning to live with your shortcomings may be the easiest way to shortchange yourself.

Bud Smith

ROOTS

*Who you are is about where you've come from
and where you are going.*

❖

*Common sense may be the most priceless
inheritance we can pass from one generation
to the next.*

*Being the first to do this or that means you
have the responsibility to work in the interest of
a second, a seventh, a nine hundredth to follow
where you pioneered.*

❖

*Parents who are at odds should remember the
African proverb: When elephants fight, it is the
grass that suffers.*

The more we pull together toward a common future, the less it matters what pushed us apart in the past.

From wherever you begin, the higher the climb, the better the view.

We had nothing to do with who our ancestors were. But we can have so much to do with who our children become.

Even when a journey has a destination, the destination may not be the main part of it all.

The deeper the roots, the taller the tree. The more you know about history, the more you can see into the future.

❖

*Remaining in touch with your people —
who they are and where they have come from —
will surely help you get to where you
need to be.*

❖

An African proverb correctly asserts that you can't know where you're going if you don't know where you've been. But let history and past experience instruct rather than determine your destination.

❖

PHILOSOPHY

Anticipating a good thing is sometimes better than the reality of it.

❖

It's amazing how few folks understand that the main thing you should do with music is to listen to it.

Like most products, quality has a shelf-life. You have to keep replenishing it.

❖

Sometimes you have to turn an idea on its head to make sure it has a good leg to stand on.

Organizations, like individuals, must be big enough to admit mistakes, smart enough to profit from them, and strong enough to correct them.

Let's get on with technology as a way of connecting us to people and places we have never known and have never seen. But let us not give up the power of plain ol' human talk to do the same.

There is no human tragedy more piercingly painful than parents burying their own child.

❖

Being full yesterday has little to do with being hungry today.

*Trying to make a way out of no way is
sometimes the only way.*

❖

*Faced with what seems like an impossible task,
a group of folks will do well to remember the
African proverb: When spider webs unite
they can tie up a lion.*

Is it not the courage of conviction that moves mountains and parts oceans?

❖

Some things are fully worth doing even if you know the final product will be far short of perfect: write a poem, sing in the shower, greet someone in their language instead of your own.

*Of course it is possible to live without the arts,
but to do so compromises the very art of living.*

❖

*There are a few possessions which once gone are
impossible to recapture. Your integrity
is one of them.*

Each of us will be known by the company we keep.

❖

Hanging out only with people who are like you is like keeping your boat in the harbor. You'll be perfectly safe, but you won't go very far in this world.

Until you've been in another's place you don't fully know your own.

Fear is the inability to put yourself in the position to see that there is nothing to fear.

WORK

Don't leave a job too soon or stay too long.

❖

Careful how you treat folks on your way up the ladder. You may well meet them on an unwanted trip down.

What matters is not what job you do but how well you do that job.

❖

At that moment when committed and concerted effort needs to take over from patience devoid of action, receive justification from an Ethiopian saying: If you wait long enough even an egg will walk.

Rushing to save time is one of the easiest ways to lose it.

❖

Although work and a job are not the same, some of us are fortunate enough to have a job that is their work.

Work well done is much more like the unfolding of a flower than the drama of a thunderbolt.

Those who doubt the centrality of work in our lives have but to be without it.

*Without work, what reason would we
have for rest?*

❖

*The best kind of work involves doing well
by doing good.*

LEADERSHIP

True, you can't get blood from a turnip, but squeeze anyhow and you just might get something.

Surround yourself with loyal but mediocre people and that's what you will get: loyal but mediocre people.

Never ask of those who report to you the performance of a task you would not be willing to do yourself.

Treat yourself whenever you can to noontimes with people who have much more on their minds than what's for lunch.

It's essential to take your responsibility seriously, but it's best not to take yourself too much that way.

❖

Leadership comes not only from growing up in a place called home, but from growing out into unfamiliar places.

Leadership is often about pointing folks in the direction they have collectively decided to take.

❖

With the mantle of leadership comes the responsibility of knowing when to be silent, and even when to stand still.

The ultimate expression of leadership is service to others.

❖

The best leaders follow their hearts as well as their heads, and they never ever leave their principles behind.

The greatest lesson a leader can teach is that life is a process, not an event.

❖

Leadership is about decisions, and the speed with which one can follow a wrong one by making one that works.

Leadership is about believing one hundred percent in yourself, and learning to believe two hundred percent in the folks you are asking to follow you.

*It is those with the boldest dreams
who awaken the best in all of us.*

President Emerita of Spelman College, Johnnetta B. Cole earned her undergraduate degree at Oberlin College and received M.A. and Ph.D. degrees in anthropology from Northwestern University. She assumed the presidency of Spelman in 1987, becoming the first African American woman to head this historically Black college for women. At Dr. Cole's inauguration, Drs. Bill and Camille Cosby made a gift of $20 million to Spelman, and for ten years Dr. Cole has led the school into the ranks of America's outstanding colleges.

A renowned author, teacher, and leader, Dr. Cole will in 1998 assume her new position as Presidential Distinguished Professor of Anthropology, Women's Studies, and African American Studies at Emory University in Atlanta, where she lives with her husband, Arthur J. Robinson, Jr.